Happy Coloring!

Heather Land
HEATHER'S ADULT COLORING BOOKS
www.facebook.com/HeatherLandBooks

Special acknowledgement to the people in **www.retailworkerconfessions.co.uk** for helping come up with the ideas in this book! If you have retail rants of your own to share or if you need to vent about your retail job, check them out!! Also, check out the book Retail Stole My Life **www.retailstolemylife.co.uk** If you work retail, you need this book!

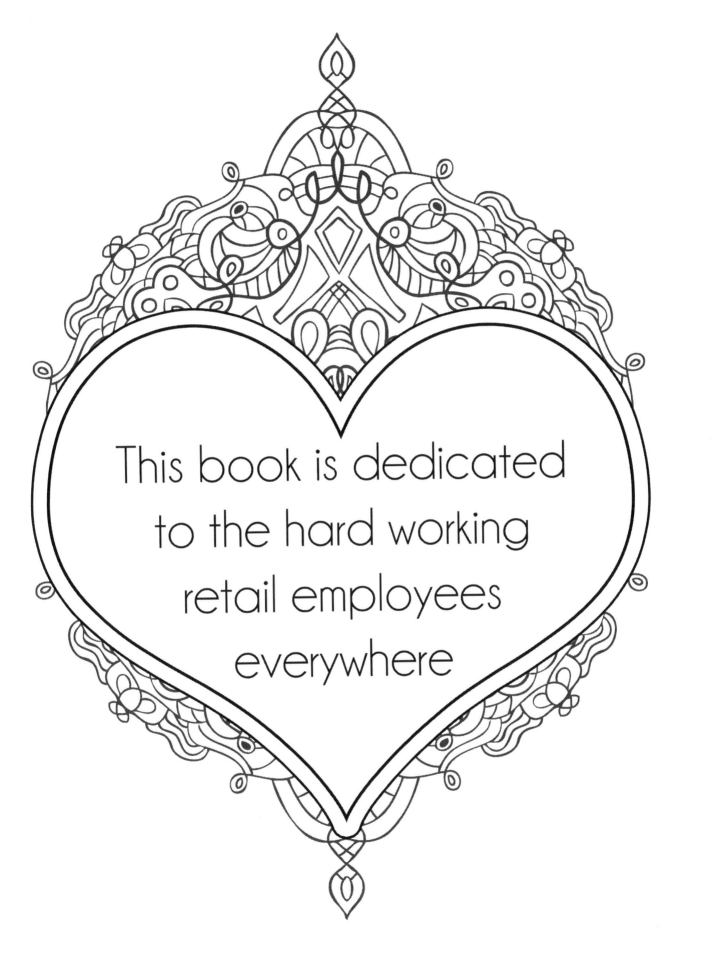

This book is dedicated
to the hard working
retail employees
everywhere

PAPER "KAREN" VOODOO DOLLS

COLOR EACH VOODOO DOLL
TO LOOK LIKE THE CUSTOMER
THAT WRONGED YOU.

THEN CUT THEM OUT,
TEAR THEM UP, CRUMPLE
THEM UP, OR BURN THEM!
DO WHATEVER YOU WANT
TO THEM TO RELIEVE
YOUR STRESS!

*These dolls are for de-stressing only. No "Karens" will actually be harmed during the destruction of these dolls. If you choose to burn them, do so at your own risk. You're responsible for your own stupidity.

NAME/DESCRIPTION: _____

NAME/DESCRIPTION: _____

NAME/DESCRIPTION:_____

NAME/DESCRIPTION:_____

NAME/DESCRIPTION: _____

COLOR TEST SQUARES

TEST YOUR COLORS HERE AND USE THIS
PAGE AS A REFERENCE GUIDE

COLOR TEST SQUARES

TEST YOUR COLORS HERE AND USE THIS
PAGE AS A REFERENCE GUIDE

Made in the USA
Columbia, SC
16 October 2023

24524567R00039